Questi(for the)ns
Possibilities

KAREN PROCTOR

TATE PUBLISHING & *Enterprises*

TATE PUBLISHING
& *Enterprises*

Tate Publishing is committed to excellence in the publishing industry. Our staff of highly trained professionals, including editors, graphic designers, and marketing personnel, work together to produce the very finest books available. The company reflects the philosophy established by the founders, based on Psalms 68:11,

"THE LORD GAVE THE WORD AND GREAT WAS THE COMPANY OF THOSE
WHO PUBLISHED IT."

If you would like further information, please contact us:

1.888.361.9473 | www.tatepublishing.com

TATE PUBLISHING & *Enterprises*, LLC | 127 E. Trade Center Terrace

Mustang, Oklahoma 73064 USA

Published in the United States of America
ISBN: 1–5988677–1-7
07.02.20

To David Fenwick and Olivia Proctor
Your love is great.

PREFACE

In a way this is a story of a little child. When we were young children the possibilities opened to us because we asked the questions. We can continue to discover life anew when we ask the questions. As for the answers? It is not so much about the answers. It is in the asking that the doors open on new worlds. It is in the living rather than the answers.

Questions for the Possibilities has arisen from my interest in life, what people find most important in life and in their lives and specifically from my work with clients who are for the most part CEOs of private and public companies. The work we do is dialogue and real learning. It is a practice I created based in British Physicist David Bohm's Learning Theory as well as in the leadership and organizational learning work out of Oxford and MIT and by William Isaacs and Peter Senge. Clients have asked that I write on this work. The simplest key to the outcomes of dialogue and real learning which is also its foundation is inquiry. There are 115 questions here.

These questions stimulate thinking. Most often we do not make the time in our hectic lives to do the thinking that would bring these questions to mind. Included are my responses which I hope may be both interesting to you and provide stimulus for new thinking. Would you adapt to a future that arrives or would you help create the desired future?

Karen Proctor
Portland, Oregon
June 23, 2006

QUESTIONS

These questions are for life. We (my clients and I) have found them valuable for clarity and moving forward in life authentically as they reveal us for who we are and who we can be. If you will begin, let the questions sit, keep going, and when you've responded then take a look at the responses I have given as a personal example, you are likely to gain the greater value. If you'd like to share your responses with me please email knproctor@gmail.com and a new conversation may begin.

"Only Connect."
    —E.M. Forster

If I group these questions for you they fall out in three basic areas...

Our Questions Related to Ourselves

Our Questions Related to Others

Our Questions Related to Life

Our Questions Related to Ourselves

When do you feel most alive?

What do you want? Why is this question important?

What has been the major motivating factor in your life? If it has changed, what was it and what is it now?

What have you been given that was of significant value, that is of significant value? Why was it, why is it of value?

What is your gift?

What are you giving?

What is most important to you?

What do you believe?

What are your deepest held beliefs? What do your beliefs mean for your life?

What do you think about?

Where is all this (from all the previous questions) bringing you?

What 5 things do you like to do most? Why?

At what can you be the best in the world?

What makes you cry? Why?

What 8 to 10 words and a couple of short phrases would you use to describe yourself to someone, if your objective was to have this person begin to really know you?

What do you like doing least? Why?

What bothers or annoys you?

What disappoints you most in life?

What do you consider your finest accomplishment?

What is your favorite book? Why?

What is your favorite color? Smell? Taste? Touch? Sound? Flower? Sight?

What are your strengths?

Where do you believe your strengths are meant to bring you?

Our Questions Related to Others

What do you value most in people? Why?

Whom do you admire? Why?

Whom do you love? Why?

Whom do you respect? Why?

Whom do you trust? Why?

If you could share two hours with anyone who would it be? Why?

What may we observe in others that is most interesting?

What may we observe in others that is most valuable?

Our Questions Related to Life

Do you seek to be liked? If yes, what effect is this having on your actions and therefore over time, your direction?

If making a choice between being liked or being respected may be important, why might it be and what is your choice? Why?

What are the ramifications of acting from the premise of being respected?

What don't you do?

What is your time bringing?

What does your time bring others?

Why do you spend your time as you do?

Can an equation be made between time and life? What equation would you draw?

Do you use the phrase to "kill time" or "killing time"? Why?

What is most important?

Do dogs make you smile? If yes, why?

Do you paint? Have you tried?

What is a valuable key to give a person early in life, to help them find their way? Why would you give this key?

If you could pass a few pearls of wisdom to the children of the world what would you give them?

Who would be your first choice as neighbors on either side of where you live?

For what are you willing to die?

What is your purpose?

Do you see your approach to life; that is the point from where you begin with your internal conversations, interactions with others and how you see the world? How might you describe your approach?

How might you begin to see your approach more clearly? What may be the value in seeing the point from where you begin all?

Are you willing to see reality?

Do you engage with reality?

Where will engaging other than with reality bring you?

Why do you think pride is one of the seven deadly sins?

Have you noticed that people have vastly different capacities to love? What does this mean in life?

Does love die when you die?

What is reflection?

Do you reflect? If yes, what does it mean or bring you? If no, why?

If there are two kinds of reflection what are they?

What does our language say about us?

Have you reflected upon the words "Know Thyself"? If so, what do they mean in your life? If not, why?

If there are two levels of listening what are they?

What does voice tell us?

What is confidence?

If there are two kinds of confidence what are they?

How would you characterize a good leader?

Are you a leader? Is it important to be a leader, in any way? Why?

What is the most important thing you can do for your children? For children?

What is the value of silence?

What value do you place on character, your own and that of others?

What is the difference between character and personality?

What is more important to you, character or personality? Why?

What does this say about you?

What might be learned from how you think about the difference between personality and character?

Why does something become classic, for example a book, piece of music, a painting?

What holds intrinsic value?

What lasts?

How does one uncover true purpose?

When someone builds a house, a family, a museum, a life why do some build to have it last?

What are your motives? Do you note motives of others? Why?

Do your conversations uncover you? Why? Do you gain a chance to discover the other person in your conversations? Why?

Do your conversations move you forward? Why?

What do you give?

What is the root of the word intelligence?

Why did Einstein invite his neighbors over for tea?

What is wisdom?

How do we create new thinking?

Can you describe how you learn?

How do we learn together?

Would you rather adapt to time and life or help create your future? Why? What is the difference?

What is the difference between being an adaptive learner and a real learner in life?

What is the difference between training, education and learning?

Do you engage openly? Why?

Are honesty and openness linked? If so, how?

Do you ask the big questions? Of yourself, of others? Why?

Do you read? Why do you read what you read?

Do you write?

What is the value in reading and writing? How may we add to the value?

Why don't you go to the movies?

What is your dream?

Do we have an impact on life? On the world? Why?

Have you ever taken a leap of faith? Why? Why not?

For what are you waiting? Why are you waiting?

Are you ambitious for something? Do you have ambition to something? What is the difference in life between being ambitious for something and having ambition to something? What value to you place on ambition?

Do you compete? Do you compete against others? With yourself? Why? What is the difference? What is the difference in terms of direction in life?

What is the difference in terms of direction in life between a focus on competing and a focus beyond what currently exists?

Have you uncovered your purpose?

Are you uncovering your visions?

What is the difference between a vision and a goal?

What is the difference between a vision and purpose?

What was the difference between Churchill and Hitler?

What differentiates lives?

Is there good and evil?

Is life worth moving from a short-term to a long-term perspective?

What questions would you ask?

RESPONSES

The responses to the questions are grouped based on whether the direction of the response is primarily from myself, others, or life. Of course all the questions are for life.

Our Response to Ourselves

Q When do you feel most alive?

Outdoors with people who are authentic, just being themselves, dancing, singing, thinking, reading, writing, laughing, with dogs and children, with animals and amongst the trees, in good conversation.

Q What do you want? Why is this question important?

I want to fully live life and this translates as sharing life every day. Specifically this means engaging authentically and being open to offer and receive. I want to learn, be approachable, be present in the moment, be gracious. I want freedom. Without freedom can we be fully alive to life? I want to make my decisions in life under God. I really want a dog. I could say I think I want a bright, open, somewhat cozy house in a beautiful temperate spot with privacy and trees and some land. Yet this one I'm a bit unsure about. Since it is not yet apparent as to whether and when I am to work with orphans I do not truly know if this house is what I want . . . perhaps in the short term.

This is an important question because what we really want is where we are headed. When you look at what you want, do you like where you are headed?

Q What has been the major motivating factor in your life? If it has changed what was it and what is it now?

It had been doing what I want, to adventure. Now it is a deep sense of responsibility for the gift of life given.

Q What have you been given that was of significant value, that is of significant value? Why was it, why is it of value?

The love I was given as a child from my parents was real love. This offered real confidence for living life fully, pursuing purpose and having a foundation of love from which to offer others. I have been given love as God gives and faith in God and love.

Q What is your gift?

A gift of faith, joy and discernment.

Q What are you giving?

Openness and, therefore, who I am and the chance of a real and ongoing conversation with life.

Q What is most important to you?

God, freedom, one's purpose, family, people, truth, character, courage, good health.

Q What do you believe?

That our character is who we are at our deepest level. That our choices outline our character to be seen for the looking. That there is good and evil. That life is not about me. That we have a purpose under God. That life is ultimately valuable as we are created by God. That if we can see that our thinking significantly affects what direction our lives take we understand a great truth that will impact our lives and those of others.

Q What are your deepest held beliefs? What do your beliefs mean for your life?

That God listens ever so closely to our hearts. That he is ever present for us if we will but ask for him. That if we will seek a relationship and an ever closer relationship with him our lives will be as they are meant. That at the end of this life it is just he and we or as Martin Buber puts it, "I and Thou." He calls the life he gave before him and then we will see where we sit at his table.

Q What do you think about?

Human character and motivation, the whys in people's lives and what really matters and in light of the end, who God would have us be and what he would have us do.

Q Where is this (from all the previous questions) bringing you?

It has brought me my work, my direction, insight and a sense that life is a great adventure and we are meant to learn as children do, in the real sense, all life long. If I will persist and be consistent it will bring me to where God's plan is best realized.

Q What five things do you like to do most? Why?

1. Be outdoors and with a friend. Why? The quiet and serenity of the outdoors provides for the simplest enjoyment and if along with a game of tennis or a walk and talk there is not much that is better.

2. Be with animals. Why? Animals bring joy because they are open, pure of motive, unencumbered by agenda.

3. Read. Why? It is enlivening. It opens doors to worlds unknown. It is enlightening, and calming which then places one in the best frame from which to clearly think, be, explore and understand what is important. Through reading one becomes more discerning. You may open a book in the middle and by reading just a few paragraphs see something of the author's thinking process. Is there real learning here? It is firstly the author's passion and interest in his topic and therefore his concentrated energy, focus and understanding in and of life that engages me. This and the offer of a journey with the imagination is what offers great reward.

4. Engage in good conversation. Why? Good conversation is alive and comes from people being real, here there is real learning, truth and life.

5. Learn. To learn in the real sense, is to be fully alive and growing, drawing the connections between people and reality, moving in life, living life.

Q At what can you be the best in the world?

Myself.

Q What makes you cry? Why?

Nobleness in the human heart, human endeavor that strives in courage in expression of responsibility to life and therefore to God moves me most. Injustice, truth, courage, the simplicity of human warmth and caring, understanding and being understood makes me cry. Understanding and being understood is an uncovering, a recognition that in a moment in time you see and are seen. In this there is a great closeness to another person. If one is interested in life, that is in meaning beyond oneself, this draws one closer to those with whom understanding also exists. This can happen too when reading and one makes the discovery that someone else, the writer, has understood something that you also understand, appreciate and value.

Q What 8 to 10 words and a couple of short phrases would you use to describe yourself to someone, if your objective was to have this person begin to really know you?

I would write: A deep faith in God, respect for fine character, reflective, strong, determined, energetic, impatient, conceptualizer, interested in the truth, no time for dishonesty and little time for non-openness, with some ambition.

Q What do you like doing least?

Minute time-absorbing tasks

Q What bothers or annoys you?

Noise, selfish people for they are great life wasters, poor service, and these three are related.

Q What disappoints you most in life?

People who do not properly appreciate the gift of life they have been given and these are people who swim in the pool of non-transcendent objectives. If there are two pools in which to swim in life there is the pool of service which sources from a deep-seated sense of responsibility to life and others and if we're lucky and have courage, we love the way in which we are expending our time. Then there is the other pool where what we do with life has not to do with much beyond ourselves. Swimming here, we do not give ourselves the chance of finding work we can love, of creating a life to love and we shortchange everyone with whom we have anything to do. Work is often for an objective other than directly related to a true interest. Everyone we encounter in life is affected by the pool in which we choose to swim. As a practical example if you are administering a patient because you love being a nurse or a doctor, your patient receives the kind of care that is most appreciative of life. This holds true for any work in which we engage and for any contact we have. Do we ask the question, "Where does our swim lead?"

Q What do you consider your finest accomplishment?

My relationship with David.

Q What is your favorite book? Why?

Alexandre Dumas's *The Count of Monte Cristo*. Because the character of the protagonist is fine in the classic sense of this word. The substance of the Count's character describes the essence of a life invested in life itself. This depiction of character makes crystalline why we must know, if we are to truly live, for what we are willing to die.

Q What is your favorite color? Smell? Sound? Touch? Taste? Flower? Sight?

Green. Flowers, grass, cedar trees, pine trees. David's voice, the quiet of nature, birds singing, my nieces voices, a beautiful piece of classical music. Soft, used Egyptian cotton, flower petals, lambs ears. Cookie batter, fresh berries and chocolate. Sweet peas, gardenias, forsythia, mimosa, lilacs, plumeria, long purples, mauve stock. Thick-trunked big trees, green grass, open sunlit sky, sun shining in big clean windows, a baby grand piano in a great room, wall to wall floor to ceiling dark rich thick wood shelves housing a good library, a smiling child running to be with you, a loved one, a dog running and jumping to greet you, classic paintings and architecture.

Q What are your strengths?

Deep interest in life. Energy. Interest in learning. An ability to conceptualize. Insight and foresight. A gift of discernment. Joy in life. Lack of cynicism.

Q Where do you believe your strengths are meant to bring you?

To connect. To love. To give. To share God.

Our Response to Others

Q What do you value most in people? Why?

It used to be that I valued "interesting." I came to learn that once fascination evaporated in the shallows, the real interest lay in the depths. To understand the depths one must look to character. The character that I value is outlined in honesty, openness and self-knowledge, an awareness and interest in life, courage, and an understanding of God. If one is not open, how can one be seen, how can life be shared? If one is not open, is one honest? In encounters, in conversations what are we offering? If we are not open, are we even offering ourselves?

Q Whom do you admire? Why?

I admire Winston Churchill. He prepared himself all life long for the call. As William Shakespeare wrote, "the readiness is all" (*Hamlet*, Act V Scene II). Churchill's courage, determination, depth of understanding and foresight, along with faith to follow it through, has been seldom paralleled. I admire the disciplined reflection that provided him insight. The homework he did all life long in pursuit of serving his calling; the British people and the peoples of the world who would live in liberty in his time and for posterity are his legacies. I admire one who has such a deep interest in life. Why does Liberty hold such intrinsic value? Liberty affords us the employment of the free will we have been given to determine the course of our lives. He valued liberty as I do. He understood the cost and readied himself for the payment.

Q Whom do you love? Why?

In the beginning I loved Mom and Dad and then my brother. Then there was my grandmother and my dogs and horse. Then there was David. Then I learned how much I loved God. Now I love my nieces. There is love for friends, for my country, for little children and in some wonderful way for all the peoples of the world.

Q Whom do you respect? Why?

Someone who is the same with everyone attracts my respect because this is someone who understands that we are all created equal. One who possesses a sense of responsibility to life and therefore to the creator, is someone to respect. David, because the generous expression of his finest characteristics is consistent.

Q Whom do you trust? Why?

In general I trust people unless my sense tells me otherwise. I trust two friends to their core because of their character.

Q If you could share two hours with anyone who would it be? Why?

My father, who passed away in 1987, would be the one. The depth of his love enabled him to know me well and was evident in the respect and wisdom he displayed in standing back to see me. As a result he gave, if asked, the best advice and he offered the best environment within which to blossom. I have seen his insight and understanding realized in the discovery of my life. How great it would be to sit down with him and learn what he would say now. The gift (of life) when seen as such, and offered openly is, when received, the example of being alive in life.

Q What may we observe in others that is most interesting?

Character is most interesting because this is our core; this is from where all comes. This speaks to who we are, where we are going, who we will be.

Q What may we observe in others that is most valuable?

Character, it is what lasts and it is the truest picture of the heart.

Our Response to Life

Q Do you seek to be liked? If yes, what effect is this having on your actions and therefore over time, your direction?

I don't tend to seek to be liked. If I am seeking to be liked am I adapting rather than creating my life and future? Being liked may be just a result of fitting in, requiring no development on my part. Is this good for life, is it a good example to give, encouraging the acceptance of the same in another? Acting from a motivation of being liked is adapting to another or to an environment. Much more character development is required to see and have the courage to be oneself, whether another likes you or not. Therein lies the way to living life truly. If one is consistent in the mission to be true to one's gift of life, real movement in life results. This then is a real gift one gives to life, to others. That is, the gift is in the actualized life as given and also, in the example.

Q If making a choice between being liked or being respected may be important, why might it be and what is your choice? Why?

Our Dad told me when I was about thirteen you have to decide early in life whether you want to be liked or respected. I'm thankful that I decided respect was more important. There always comes a time when your actions will be directed by your motivation in this regard, whether being liked or being respected is more important, and the outcome of your actions will pivot on the motivation. If I am respected it is a reflection of an understanding of who I am and a reflection of a true connection with another. If we operate with a premise of seeking to be liked we relegate our self to going along with what is acceptable to others and in so doing choose in some way the other's path, leaving our own undiscovered. Is this comparable to not stepping up to bat, to defaulting and handing the bat to someone else? If we add up all our days then the entire game was defaulted. If everyone acts like this what life are we living here? What does it all mean if we are unwilling to try our ground, temper our steel or exercise our self to learn who we really are? Does it mean that at the end, when there is no more time left we won't know who we are? Does it mean that you let your end down? That all the others with whom you lived at that moment in time did not even know you? "This above all, to thine own self be true; and it must follow as the night the day, thou canst not then be false to any man" (Shakespeare, *Hamlet*, Polonius Act I scene III).

Q What are the ramifications of acting from the premise of being respected?

We will more likely live as who we truly are. In so doing we offer a true gift to others in the giving of ourselves and of the example. We are not ourselves if we would trade our truth for a measurement of acceptance. It must be far more rewarding, even if but at the deepest level, to live as who we are than be a stranger to ourselves. I'd like to be able to look in the mirror each morning and recognize the reflection. At the end of the day when all the people whom we might have sought after go home, we can know who we are and be the best example we can be.

Q What don't you do?

I do not walk through a door ahead of an elderly person. I do not ignore others in close proximity. I do not make loud noises if it can at all be helped. I try not to use a cell phone on the street or in a small public place.

Q What is your time bringing?

My time is bringing a sense that my direction is true. It is bringing more and yet perhaps never complete satisfaction with work that has evolved to be more truly a reflection of strengths and deep interests. Also it is bringing greater understanding of life, others and true purpose. Time is showing me lasting and dear friendships. Time is bringing greater peace within, a closer relationship with and deeper love of God and knowledge of life and death.

Q What does your time bring others?

My time is bringing others love, friendship, care, some insight. I would like my time to bring others more understanding, respect, kindness and a lot more love.

Q Why do you spend your time as you do?

How do I spend my time? I rise early, preferably 5:30 AM, this is much easier in the Spring and Summer, because the day feels one's own early in the morning. After thirty minutes of stretching-type exercises I go outdoors for a walk. Each weekday morning I make phone calls to clients and prospective clients. Client sessions are usually in the afternoons. Most of my day is spent alone and while I have pondered this aspect of my life a number of times, over time there is something in it that I must like very much. Late in the day I want to be reading while there is still natural light. My friendships are one to one and we keep them through conversations on a regular irregular basis. My friends are in different phases of life including a teenager and two who are 90 years. Sometimes we take trips to meet up. On Sunday nights my friend Bruce in New York and I get on the phone together and go over the chapters in the Bible we had designated for our weekly reading. Now this is obviously the life of a single person. I wonder at the change if I were sharing life ongoing with a husband? Now with children ...

While I am thankful to be living the life I choose, I'm continually checking to learn if it is the best way to invest time, and what may be a better way. I sense that the path is true, and that the visions appear and become clear with continued tuning.

Q Can an equation be made between time and life? What equation would you draw?

Yes. Time equals Life.

Q Do you use the phrase to "kill time" or "killing time"? Why?

No. Time is life.

Q What is most important?

God, people, family, character, one's purpose, freedom, courage, truth

Q Do dogs make you smile? If yes, why?

Oh yes. Dogs are direct, pure in their approach. They are naturally completely open to what is before them, not hidden in their response. Oh that people were more like this!

Cats in contrast are often self-interested and this place from which they come often directs sly behavior. Where a cat will wait in hiding to pounce on a bird, a dog will chase a squirrel, openly announcing for the world to see his intention of fun. Have you registered how dogs greet each other? Like young children, and even more so, they run up to one another in eager anticipation of exploring and learning and in hopes of finding a friend. What purer expression of the joy of life is there? Also, dogs give an insight into their master. If a dog is not open to respond, unless ill, this natural response has been snuffed out of him. Who then is his master?

Q Do you paint? Have you tried? Why?

Once as a young teenager I tried with oils to paint the likeness of a woman. Winston Churchill, who painted, said that to keep the mind active in a wholly different way is the best rest. I'd like to make the attempt again with more commitment.

Q What is a valuable key to give a person early in life, to help them find their way? Why would you give this key?

Know thyself (Socrates and the Delphi Oracle). One must uncover oneself, one's gift of life that one may lead the life meant to be.

Beginning work early in life on the homework entailed in "Know Thyself" one may best see the relationship one is meant to have with one's maker, with others and with the world.

My father gave me "Know Thyself." Have you noticed that when we do our own homework, we are in a better position to see others and be present for them? "Observe all men; thy self most" (Benjamin Franklin.) There is an additional necessary element for the whole to work, the element is service. Know thyself that you are positioned to be yourself and in so being you provide the true gift to others, service and the offer of the example. It is not about "me."

Q If you could pass a few pearls of wisdom to the children of the world what would you give them?

Pray and work on a closer relationship with God. Read the Bible. Read the classics. Be outdoors. First know thyself. Then be yourself. Give all you have to give. Love God, feel your responsibility to your creator, to the gifts he gave you and develop your relationship with him and look to find true relationships with others. Be courageous. Focus on what has meaning and really matters. If possible try and get a good liberal arts education in history and literature and or philosophy and another language.

Q Who would be your first choice as neighbors on either side of where you live?

Steffi Graf on one side and David Suchet on the other.

Q For what are you willing to die?

For the freedom we have been given to live the life we have been given.

Q What is your purpose?

To have as personal a relationship with God as possible. To be myself, be whom he has made me to be and the best of that and to share this life for his purpose.

Q Do you see your approach to life, that is, the point from where you begin with your internal conversations, interactions with others and how you see the world? How might you describe your approach?

I try to see my own approach by cultivating awareness and employing thinking. I see that the strong awareness I have could be better utilized if my strong impatience could be neutralized. Also, a quick mind may invest its extra energy more productively if judgments are quickly identified and suspended. My approach is open, aware, impatient, inquiring, interested in understanding the whole picture (unless to do with family in which case my emotions may get the better of me) and in seeing the key elements that the connections may be drawn to see the whole picture. Listening is vastly improved when I will suspend assumptions that I may be more open to awareness and breathe into impatience.

Q How might you begin to see your approach more clearly? What may be the value in seeing the point from where you begin all?

Is it of value to see the point from where we begin each thought, interaction and action, the point from where we are directed? Yes, because by understanding that we can observe our approach, our very starting point, we can move our lives. By looking to our starting point we offer ourselves the opportunity of understanding. Understanding is an impetus that moves us and therefore life. Do you know that your view of whether you impact the world around you affects the future?

Q Are you willing to see reality?

Yes. This is what leads us in light into the future.

Q Do you engage with reality?

Yes, because otherwise we are stuck in a nether land while life moves on. When reality is not faced what we are doing is building a wall against life and keeping ourselves prisoners instead of being free to live completely.

Q Where will engaging other than with reality bring you?

To a dead stop.

Q Why do you think pride is one of the seven deadly sins?

Pride results in non-openness and therefore a dishonesty. It breaks relationships; it stops us from asking for help, from engaging with others, it cuts us off and offers less for others. It stops life. God dislikes pride most because he wants a relationship with us and he wants us to love. How can we love if we will not show who we are? Pride is most dangerous and costly as it is the greatest hindrance to our true purpose.

Q Have you noticed that people have vastly different capacities to love? What does this mean in life?

Yes. The direction of life is immutably fixed by whether we engage with real love or no. Herein lies the importance of seeing the difference between real love and the counterfeit. If you will not choose to give or seek to enable yourself to give real love, you will miss the key to life and everlasting life. It means that if you have a capacity for real love you may have a hard time finding a match. Real love has not to do with what you want; it has to do with that beyond yourself.

A Story . . .
One day, I must have been eight, my Dad came home with a brand new beautiful red bicycle. It was a complete surprise; it was my first bike and I had not asked for it. He handed it to me outside the front of our house and said, "This is yours." He turned and walked back to the house. "Aren't you going to help me?" I asked. "That's your bike," he said, and was in the house. I stood there holding onto the handlebars and tears came to my eyes. I remember feeling that my Dad was being mean not helping me. However, all I was seeing was the present moment magnified. As I stood kind of struck dumb and motionless holding tightly to the handlebars, something happened. I started to struggle to think. I didn't know how to ride a bike. I didn't want to give up the bike. What was I going to do? I'd seen kids my age riding these two wheelers. It could be done. I faced the bike and tried to climb onto it struggling with the thought

that I did not understand how it and I were going to stay up and move forward. I fell, the bike fell and it likely got its first scratch. After a number of tries, I think I got maybe two and a half pedals in and fell again. Those few moments though, moving with the bike, were exhilarating. The next thing I remember I was zooming around the crescent. There was no one else there. It must have been a week night and likely everyone else was in for dinner. I wonder now if Dad had told Mom that I was out there and to let me continue with my adventure. The feeling I had as I zoomed around the crescent came from somewhere beyond the learning of bike riding. I wasn't riding, I was flying and while I couldn't articulate it then, I was flying with the knowledge that I could figure it out, I could do things and importantly, on my own. Years and years later, maybe somewhere in my thirties, in thinking about this I realized that that day my Dad had given me something far beyond a bicycle. He had given me the love that looks beyond today, the love that speaks again to us across time. Instead of having fun himself in playing, watching and helping me, he knew that someday he would not be there and I'd have to face something bigger on my own.

Some give love unreservedly, not for a reason to do with themselves. If we have real love to give and give it, others are enabled. People having different capacities to love also means that to come home you must find where your love meets its match. This is true with regards to a match with another person and everywhere in life. My observation is that the love that people often give, know and give, is self-centered instead of real, sourcing beyond themselves. Is the reason that God has most of us have children because most of us would not reach real love without them, to glimpse real love, have the chance to know real love and then give it to others? If love is real it will overflow into all of life. Yet it too often does not overflow to others. Why does one not go deeper? Why may we remain content, unto ourselves? Why do many not extend their love beyond their circle? If we do not extend love beyond our circle, is it real love? If we will not give beyond our circle, how can the love we give within our circle be real?

Q Does love die when you die?

No, love does not die if you love in the real sense. "God is love" (I John 4:8 KJV). Do you understand how one can spend, and this is spendy, his or her life loving someone and not think that love itself, God, is worth deciding about? If we do not decide for him are we not deciding against our own life and love? What will happen to your love if you do not believe in eternity? What is the value you place on your gift of life and your love if you would not look to give your love eternal value?

Q What is reflection?

Reflection is an exercise of the mind. To reflect is to think for ourselves. It is to see more and more clearly. To reflect is to see ourselves as we are and as we have been given to be, a foundation from which to begin to see others. It is to think about approach in life including thinking process. How do we take in and then digest reality? We reflect if we want to see the meaning. To reflect is to digest that to which our awareness gives attention. Reflection is to look again, anew, to apply thinking to others and ones own actions, words and motives. As we practice, our reflection will have us see more clearly and more deeply into life.

Q Do you reflect? If yes, what does it mean or bring you? If no, why?

Yes. My father's interaction with me and his example gave cause for reflection early in life. Reflection moves one to gain understanding. The result of reflection is the drawing of connections over time, which provides impetus to move us, to grow continuously all life long. This is how one's visions are uncovered.

Q If there are two kinds of reflection what are they?

1. You are out on the range and there isn't much to think about so you ponder something.
2. Then there is the exercise of the mind by thinking over connections made through life interactions and our own internal processes. In this way our own process, that of others, and the why's of how we see life itself and the world may be uncovered.

Q What does our language say about us?

Our language issues from our thinking, our very approach to life, and speaks to our attitude, our inlook and our outlook. If we think about why we use particular words or the way we speak to someone and then the way we speak to a different person, we can learn about ourselves. Reflecting on our choices in language will uncover our thinking and our deeper feelings. Our language portrays our worldview. It is very telling of from where we are coming. Take care of what you think about, pay attention to and study, and take care of the words you choose because our language creates a world.

Q Have you reflected upon the words "Know Thyself"? If so, what do they mean in your life? If not, why?

At about the age of seven my Dad wrote two words in my autograph book, "Know Thyself." These words became a motive force, my homework began. In some ways life became a stretch for discovery. All experiences and interactions provided material for reflection to learn more clearly what was important, to draw connections over time and gain understanding. Over time it dawned that "Know Thyself" is just the beginning homework. It is a jumping off point to those around us, the world and all that can be. Do you want to uncover who you are, who you are meant to be? It is said he who does not know himself cannot repent.

Q If there are two levels of listening what are they?

1. Listening so well that you may repeat every word and the meaning.

2. Listening so effectively that your grip on your certainties is loosened allowing room for the speaker and his views and real learning. (See Peter Senge, *The Fifth Discipline*)

Q What does voice tell us?

Ahh, what does my own voice say? What does another's voice tell me if I will but listen?

If you listen, a voice will tell you. Have you ever thought you heard the same voice over the phone at different receptions and you know she could not be in two places at the same time? Do we have an idea of how a receptionist should sound? Are we afraid to let our self out to be seen? Do we miss seeing life as a whole? Do we see life in parts, as in this is who I am at work, different from who I am at home?

Voice, if let be, portrays the true self or it will betray that we are not being ourselves. Have you heard an exuberant energy bounding out to embrace life? Have you heard a great weariness with the world, not in the words, in the tones? Have you heard a deep calm and confidence that faces the world with an awareness energized by courage to see reality? What does your voice tell you?

Q What is confidence?

Confidence is the pure simple knowledge and understanding of who you are and the deep-seated knowledge and understanding of your greatest worth and value under God. Entwined with this is a deep sense of responsibility for this sense of being and its source.

Q If there are two kinds of confidence what are they?

There is the confidence with which you are born and that is fortified through the love of those who love you deeply that is with God at heart. It grows to be deep-rooted and whole within you as in a rooted core of knowledge of one's intrinsic worth under the creator. This confidence is real confidence. It is a sense of being, more uncovered by us than created by us. It is a wellspring from which to draw all life long for living a full and purposeful life. Then there is the confidence that, if the first kind is missing, one builds over time with experience and affirmation through others. This is an acquired confidence and not as deep-rooted as the former. Since it was built from the outside it can also be disturbed from the outside. If one does not have the first kind, real, the only way to attain it is by understanding its core and going to it. The core of real confidence is a clear and deep understanding that who we are is of intrinsic value based upon our purposeful creation. This is inextricably linked to real love. If we wish to know real love we need to seek at the source. True confidence does not derive from what others think of us nor is it related to how we fair placed up against or in comparison to others. Rather it is the reverse. What others think of us is a reflection of what we think of ourselves, better, of who we are. Thus real confidence can be attained by coming to the understanding that sources in real love and then applying the courage to act upon it, of knowing oneself, being oneself and offering our self, under God.

Q How would you characterize a good leader?

A good leader is someone whose sense of purpose is apparent in the interest evident where his or her time [life] is invested. A leader stands up to take responsibility, to articulate for what he stands. He stands back to see, to learn, to engage in reflection. He stands together with others with whom he invests his time. He is always clarifying what is important and has the courage to seek to see reality clearly. His actions are characterized by a movement emanating from clear purpose. He is leading his own life. Rather than adapting to a future he is leading into and helping create a desired future. He is, with his own life, an example to others, encouraging others to be leaders of their lives and in life. This requires a deep appreciation for life. As Meg Wheatley puts it a leader is anyone willing to help.

Q Are you a leader? Is it important to be a leader, in any way? Why?

Yes, I'm a leader of my own life. Who but you can lead your life? If this can be an example that others may more clearly see to enable their purpose then together we can help enable life. We can invent our lives. When we believe we make a difference we do. Why is it important to be a leader? To help create the future and not just adapt to one that arrives, to value and appreciate the gift of life given.

Q What is the most important thing you can do for your children? For children?

Pray with them.

Q What is the value of silence?

To allow for the space that gives us the opportunity for real listening that we may be ever present in the moment given. To realize the exalted, that which exists in the space beyond words. (Paul Tillich)

Q What value do you place on character, on your own and that of others?

With regard to another person and to myself, I place the highest value on character. Character is the core, the heart of a person. Uncovered it lays bare the motives, the motive force underlying one's thoughts and deeds. It is who we are and who we will be. It is what lasts. As portrait painters are more exact in the lines of the face, in which character is seen, than in the other parts of the body (Plutarch), character can be seen in the face.

Q What is the difference between character and personality?

Personality is as the outward trappings of clothing, to be altered with the season. Character is as with a man for all seasons (see Robert Bolt's play on Sir Thomas More "A Man For All Seasons"). Character reveals the inmost depths of a man, all telling of who we are and are not. When one sees character one sees the long term.

Q What is more important to you character or personality? Why?

Character. Personality changes with the time. Character remains to be trusted over time.

Q What does this say about you?

That the long term counts. If we will be present in the moment we are in a position to see character. When we look for intention we will find it. There is intrinsic value in heeding character for time and life.

Q What might be learned from what you think about the difference between personality and character?

There is real meaning in taking an interest in learning (in Chinese "learning" means "study and practice constantly") and discovering the depths. An interest in merely being entertained will keep one on the surface and stuck in the short term. Therefore since the future arrives, one must make the decision on character and the long term or on relegating oneself to adapting to what arrives.

Q Why does something become classic, for example a book, piece of music, a painting?

A classic is something that has lasted over time because its value is timeless, indicating the presence of a depth of meaning that should be fathomed. It speaks to us in truth. The creator of the book, music or painting understood something, saw a truth and then saw the value in conveying truth. This means that there was a presence of seeing beyond oneself and an absence of self-focus and interest directed from a power motive. An example of a classic institution is the judiciary of the United States as established in the constitution. Those who have sought and who seek to influence the judicial process of a free country would take an integral element of the foundation of their country, its constitution, and that of civilization itself and undermine it. The only way to create a classic or be classic is to look to the long term with motive beyond oneself. The only way to preserve a classic is to educate ourselves on its value that we may see those who would destroy it.

Q What holds intrinsic value?

Life, real love, one's purpose in life, that which lasts, relationships based in real love, faith in God.

Q What lasts?

God, Love through eternity.

Q How does one uncover true purpose?

By looking within oneself and then beyond oneself to the whole we uncover purpose and enable long-term vision. By knowing that our purpose is under God and within us we can learn to see and uncover purpose.

Q When someone builds a house, a family, a museum, a life, why do some build to have it last?

One looks long term when one looks beyond oneself to the greater whole and purpose.

When one looks long term one becomes an enabler for that which invokes lasting value.

Q What are your motives? Do you note motives in others? Why?

My motives source from the deepest desire to follow God's road for life. I'm most curious about motives so I do note others' intentions. If you listen, look and learn over time, motives will show themselves and it is fascinating because it is all telling of direction, of the long term for lives, of who we are and will be.

Q Do your conversations uncover you? Why? Do you gain a chance to discover the other person in your conversations? Why?

Yes, conversations tend to uncover who I am and I tend to get to see others due to an open approach. A real conversation includes the classic meaning of conversation, a manner of being, a way of living. For a real conversation to take place one must be authentic, one must have the foresight and discipline to know oneself and the courage to be oneself. My friendships are based upon one to one conversations. Since most of our interactions as human beings are not magically made, and even for those that are, we must cultivate our ability to connect verbally for relationships to develop. A real connection in the long term must include an ability for real conversation. As a result of losing the made in heaven (love at first sight) connection I was offered early in life, due to a failure to verbally communicate, I decided I needed to do something about this short coming. Making myself practice for that ability to connect in the moment, that affords the possibilities longer term, I began to say out loud what I was really thinking. This exercise began in little fits and starts and then larger stumbles and bumbles. After years of practice my conversation became direct, more a flow of what I was thinking spoken aloud. Open communication is a steady process of clarifying and being open to improvement. The key is to practice and if you will practice you end up presenting yourself openly and directly and a wonderful principle of human nature comes into play people tend to respond in kind. Interactions are no longer one sided, there are no sides, exchanges become more like a flowing circle. The reward of this determined practice of saying aloud what I'm thinking rather than coloring my speech, in combination with facing the responses I get, is an insurance that the meaning of interactions is not missed and therefore that the fullness in life will be offered. This all comes from a great interest in seeing people for who they are. The result? One does get to see, and for the long term. This is from where my work, dialogue and real learning has come.

Q Do your conversations move you forward? Why?

I look for them to do so. So I try and listen for the meaning to see the other person. If a real conversation is not happening the question becomes why. Often the reason a conversation does not move is for a lack of openness. If one is not open and doesn't address reality, real movement cannot take place. The reality is that life moves. If we won't move we are left stuck and irresponsible to the gift.

Q What do you give?

Who I am, time and life. And I hope an example that we must be true to ourselves to be true to others and to life.

Q What is the root of the word intelligence?

Intelligence has two roots, from the Latin, 'Intra' meaning between, and 'Legere' meaning to gather, to gather between or illuminate, to choose between, related to wisdom. Intelligence is to gather between existing frames to create new thinking. Intelligence is that in thinking which is alive and active not past thought, which is dead.

Q Why did Einstein invite his neighbors over for tea?

He sought engagement with his neighbors to learn from that which was different from himself, to dialogue—to engage in a flow of meaning. From what I have learned he sought to learn through dialogue, how people see, feel and think. In approaching as a child, in open inquiry, he was able to see what most adults miss because they are stuck in existing systems as adaptive learners using only traditional thinking. In asking the questions Einstein saw different thinking patterns and in asking why a pattern was necessary, he could come to new thinking.

Q What is wisdom?

Is wisdom seasoned thinking that has sparked enough interest in the thinker to draw the connections over time required for insight? And then, is wisdom insight digested and used to further nourish us that sewn again, and seasoned over time, grows into ripe fruit? Just as fruit trees need nature's love (rain and sunshine) wisdom can only grow where love is.

Q How do we create new thinking?

Understanding that as adults we are engaged in traditional thinking, focused on "what currently exists" affords us the chance to begin to look to "what can be," to create new thinking. To lead into the future and help create our desired future new thinking is necessary. By recognizing a pattern and moving out of it, by stopping, pausing, reflecting on our own way of seeing and looking to learn how others see we begin to make space for new thinking. By drawing connections, relating seemingly unrelated events, people, situations, by continually clarifying what is important and continually learning to see reality more clearly, we move from traditional thinking alone and from being adaptive learners to being real learners and to new thinking and real movement in life.

Q Can you describe how you learn?

Listening, thinking, interacting, reflecting, reading. If we will be calm inside so that we can hear and listen clearly, we begin to place ourselves in position that the right string may be plucked, that the note be in tune, for another to strike the chord that the music may be played. If we can respond openly and in the moment we give others the chance to do the same. As we continue in this ever evolving learning we arrive at a new, formerly nonexistent response. This is an example of where real learning is.

Q How do we learn together?

Surely this is a hallowed position, to be learning by simultaneous connection with one another. Good ensemble theatre and excellent team sports offer this opportunity. We have this chance of learning together with whom we come into contact, if we will only connect. What will bring us here? First we must be open. This includes being open to seeing our own approach as well as that of others, from where thinking and direction come. Approach is the eye piece through which we see ourselves and others and from which comes our worldview. An open approach includes a real interest in listening and an interest in cultivating over time one's ability to listen. Where does our interest lie? Will we look beyond ourselves? Are we a family, a team? Seeing approach we can begin to understand the response we receive from people, how we impact our outcomes and our direction in life. Do we see clearly? Do we see the reality of from where we see and of how we are received? Dialoguing internally and with others leads us to clarity and to a shared vision. Seeing our approach we can begin to understand how we impact our outcomes. Do we see clearly?

Q Would you rather adapt to time and life or help create your future? Why? What is the difference?

When we adapt we are reacting to something that has occurred. If we are only using thinking from the past, we are relegating ourselves to adapting to time and life. What about creating our own system or way, one we really want? Adapting keeps us focused on the short term, on what currently exists. Therefore we are within a circle too small for the appropriate appreciation of life. How can our true abilities be uncovered by adapting? How will the music be played? What is the long-term consequence of merely adapting? I'd rather help create my future. Creating beckons our future. It calls upon who we are and asks us to give from our truest place, to arise and carpe diem. When we move from adapting to creating we offer others the best example and the opportunity to interact at the level of the whole. The difference is between helping to create and lead into life and a desired future, utilizing one's strengths and true identity, living one's life as it has been given us to live fully, in contrast to following and adapting to life as it comes, relegating one's very self to an external circumstance and a measuring stick manufactured en masse.

A story ...

This reminds me of a little break that happened for me, my beginning in breaking into acting. Do you live life by following your visions? My mind works visually. To a significant extent I have lived life by following the visions given me. So in a way it has been that I live the current vision, then I turn the knob that clicks forward to the next reel. One of these visions was a view of Central Park from my windows. This was a vision, in my mind's eye, before ever living in Manhattan or ever having even seen the view about to be described here. In this vision I could look over and down to Central Park from my windows and see the trees, the lake (which I later learned was the reservoir) and the buildings beyond to my left. Given the kind of buildings (mostly non-residential) and their position, it meant, although I did not know it at the time, that I was looking from Central Park West. This vision became reality. I found myself living in Manhattan on Central Park West. This then offered, literally, with a view of the park, the buildings and the sky, inspiration for the next vision to arise.

One of these visions was to act. At this point I had invested a decade in business. So while the logic of being an actor was hardly obvious, I embarked. After all this was New York, and wasn't New York about making one's dreams reality? Auditions were found in Backstage and I chose one that would lead to a paid part and which took place soon, while my resolve to audition remained strong. The call was 11:00 AM and I had about two and a half hours. They asked for a monologue. I checked my dictionary, yes, at least I knew what a monologue was. Then, what to do for it? A one-way phone conversation was something I could do, I used the phone a lot for work. Making something up, I practiced it a few times and went off to the audition. Arriving ten minutes ahead of time I learned that I was hours late. I placed my name in the one hundred and sixty-third spot on the list.

Actors had arranged themselves in a line beginning in the entrance hallway. They wound themselves up three flights of stairs, coming out in a large waiting area in front of the door where people entered and exited the audition. Everyone seemed to be talking to themselves, rehearsing their monologue. I tried that a few times and then wandered up and down the stairs watching the actors to see what might be learned. After a couple of hours I went up to the area where those who were soon to be called were congregating. When someone came out of the door I went up to them and asked who was behind the door and what they wanted of us. Apparently this was uncommon practice and I received blank, surprised or indignant looks. While most just ignored me a few people responded and I learned that there was just one person behind that door waiting for us, a man, of about 55 years who simply asked you to begin. This little bit of information put me more at ease.

When it was my turn I entered a huge stark gray room, like a warehouse with high rafters for ceilings. There he was sitting behind a table and there was one other chair about twenty feet out in front of him. I went up to him and extending my hand introduced myself. He said hello but just looked at me and did not extend his hand. I asked his name. He said he was Fred. He gestured to the chair and said, "Begin." I went and got the chair, pulling it up to be much closer to him so we could see each other better. He interrupted me about half way through my monologue saying he had my style, "intense," and thanked me. Since I did not intend to leave, having practiced for 2 hours, I suggested that he needed to hear the whole thing. He let me finish and when I had he asked for my resume. I didn't have one and told him so. He paused and stared. This was an audition for television, "Did I have a photo?" This I had. He looked at my full color shot and flipped it over. He took a good look at me again and asked, "Do you have a telephone number?" in a tone of such uncertainty as to indicate he was beginning to wonder if I lived on this planet. I rushed forward, took his pen and wrote in large lettering my number on the back of the photo. It was time to go. As I took his hand again and shook it for the second time he just stared. I thanked him as I backed out of the room smiling and saying I looked forward to hearing from him. I did hear from him, I got a small part.

A number of years of acting later I was able to guess that when he went back to that large pile of resumes and photos on his desk and tried to recall who was who, he could not forget our unique experience together.

I had been certain I wanted to help create the outcome and therefore would not adapt to a recognized order of things. As a result I moved the outcome and in this case, to the credit side of the ledger.

Q What is the difference between being an adaptive learner and a real learner in life?

Adapting has us relegate ourselves to a preposition, "to." We adapt "to something," so we wait for that something, for example change, and we follow. What is the value of setting our life to follow a path set by another when we can create together the future we desire? As adaptive learners we are adapting our very selves to existing systems, at work, at home and internally. We do not see the patterns within which we are stuck and miss the chance of seeing new opportunities, directions and importantly the true direction for life. If we are learning openly, our vision will be uncovered to us and our direction unfolded before us. Real learning has the long term in focus. Our visions become clarified and we can expand our ability to create, be who we are meant to be and offer this example to others. As we move from adaptive learning to real learning we leave a focus of solely traditional thinking, thereby providing space for new thinking. The result is real movement in life.

Q What is the difference between training, education and learning?

Training is instruction and includes molding. As such it may threaten creativity and the rich development that comes from looking other than to prescribed dictates. An education is more often an accreditation and perhaps an accumulation of knowledge. It is less often about learning. We learn when we listen, explore and think for ourselves. Our education system in the last 40 years has been less about thinking for ourselves (see Lengthened Shadows, editor Roger Kimball) than molding us to fit. It is to the point where the practice of thinking is seriously in jeopardy. When we learn to think, we can expand our understanding, give ourselves the chance to conceptualize, to create together, explore with others and truly expand our lives. When we have digested for ourselves what is important we can add the understanding gained with that of others and help create something that formerly did not exist. This is real learning.

Q Do you engage openly? Why?

Yes this is the only way to see what is true and to move with and in life. It is where the life is, and where the fun begins!

Q Are honesty and openness linked? If so, how?

Honesty and openness are inextricably linked. One is not wholly honest without being open. If we are not open we are hiding and then the question must be asked, why? We cannot be who we truly are without applying the courage to be, and therefore to let who we are be seen. This speaks to the value of freedom. Do we see that we have been given to be free? Without recognizing this and being determined to live free we cannot be what we have been given to be. We leave ourselves to be yoked by man and his self-interest and lack of honesty.

Q Do you ask the big questions? Of yourself, of others? Why?

Yes, the big questions, which include the what, who and why questions, are the questions most worth asking. In asking the big questions of others we offer respect for another's time and our contact with them.

Q Do you read? Why do you read what you read?

Yes, I love to read. I love to learn from reading a variety of authors, types of literature and periods in time. History provides perspective on character, the ways of man. We, as human beings, tend to some of the same basic traits over time. We want change only if it doesn't look like too much upset. We fear moving from the status quo if it means our comfort is to be disrupted and our courage required. We look to the short term, locally i.e. to our comfort now, missing or avoiding and seemingly not specifically interested in the long term significance of directions taken today, on our tomorrows or that of posterity. I love to read an author, on any subject, if he thinks for himself, has the courage to be in close touch with reality, can conceptualize and has a strong sense of responsibility to the truth.

Q Do you write?

I'm learning.

Q What is the value in reading and writing? How may we add to the value?

Learning. When we read we expose ourselves to unknowns. When we think for ourselves we add to the value. As Shakespeare had Hamlet contemplate being or not being, may we include learning or not learning? If we will not learn, and in the real sense, do we forfeit even the chance of being? Ah the unknown . . . if Hamlet had taken the leap of faith earlier, if he had adventured forth, would his life have been the tragedy it was? Shakespeare shows us the great tragedy that we may learn. The unknown . . . "the undiscovered country" from where no traveler returns, meaning that we would often far rather remain with what we know than venture to what is unknown. And what is lost? To be what we would be, our very selves? To miss the purpose, perhaps the very purpose of our lives? Certainly we will miss the fullest sense of being alive. If the writer has true interest in his subject there is truth there. Are we not the co-authors of our lives? When we move from verbal expression and commit our thinking to paper we see more of what is important to us and let others see more of us too. Worlds are opened. It is an adventure as an investment in the future of your life and the future of life. Reading and writing will help uncover your direction and create your future. Multiply this by all the people here. If we will think on our choice of what we read and then engage with the writer as we read, thinking for ourselves, and together with the other, real value is created.

Q Why don't you go to the movies?

I go to learn, to laugh and to think about what someone else has learned. I don't go when those with their offering are not thinking beyond themselves and don't have faith in love and eternity and are therefore not serving those whom they would ask to spend their time and money. Since I make the connection between time and life, and our money if earned is a representation of both, I seek to find a match. Rather than spend my time and life I seek to invest it.

Q What is your dream?

To actualize that which God has given. To realize and actualize here for the step into eternity.

Q Do we have an impact on life? On the world? Why?

Certainly we have a significant impact on life, and particularly so when we think we do. When we think the reverse that we don't affect what's going on in us and around us, we throw up our hands accepting and expecting what is and don't move to act and so our thinking helps create reality. It all begins right here and if we are consistent over time in our thinking and actions, we affect ourselves, each other, our neighbors, community and the multiplier effect out into the world more quickly and with greater impact than we may imagine. A simple example that we may all have experienced is the rumor mill. If we truly do not want something known, we must keep it to ourselves. For by acting with just one other, almost anyone, by telling them, the news or rumor will spread and given little time will take on a life of its own. Thinking in a wholly different direction the rumor mill can become the grape-vine. We have a huge impact when we act. So if we will think and source from auspices beyond ourselves, with the long term in mind, we can benefit ourselves and posterity.

Two stories . . .

One Saturday I asked my parents if I could bring my brother to the stables where my horse was kept. Would they drop us off and pick us up later in the day? They agreed and Paul, who was not quite 3, joined his 11-year-old sister for an adventure. I explained to Paul as I was brushing Chaparral that we could ride on her. I hoisted him on to her back and climbed up behind him. Expecting a slow walk about, I used only her lead rope attached to the halter. Chaparral was a calm, well-mannered horse and she and I had an easy rapport. We entered the area where the horses were, fenced from the stables and road. While I knew nothing of the herd behavior of horses, I did vaguely recognize that there was a leader, a large white shawed male horse. I saw it happen. I had seen the stable keeper's dog bark at and harass the white horse before. He came into the area and began bark-ing and nipping at the white horse's heels. The dog didn't bother us. But he got that white horse excited enough to bolt. Immediately other horses started to follow at a gal-lop. Then within a few more moments, so did Chaparral. I didn't understand why she was doing this. Somehow I thought she'd do as I asked her, as she always had done.

There were a lot of horses galloping all in the same direction, towards the woods. They were drawing closer in together and this was not a safe place for us. Besides I had had no intentions of moving so quickly with Paul and without a bridle. I was going to have to pull Paul off the horse with me. I sensed right away that it was important for me to be calm, otherwise Paul might panic and it would be harder to pull him off. Looking ahead I realized we had to get off the horse before we got to the woods. Some of the trees were not far enough apart to allow for Chaparral and us to pass. I figured that we could fall safely and I was praying that any horses behind us would be far enough back that they would skirt us. Ahead I saw a bit of a snowdrift on the ground. I told Paul that we were going to get off the horse and that when I counted one, two, three, he must let go and I would pull him off. I coaxed his acceptance. He gave me, "Okay." I knew he would be safe as long as he didn't cling to the mane. I saw us in my mind's eye a moment beforehand as pulling Paul into me in a way that my back would protect him from any hooves. We fell on the snowdrift and the horses passed us by, we both were fine.

I think I knew even then that we help create our lives. Keeping my head, thinking and acting, allowed for the outcome to be altered.

Another example is that for our speech in high school I chose as my topic the Berlin Wall. This seemed an important topic and more than deserved being voiced. Afterwards I prayed that the Wall would come down. I learned much later that others had this prayer. Then someone in a good position to be heard by many, President Reagan, spoke out loud asking that the wall be brought down.

We have more impact on life than we often can imagine.

Q Have you ever taken a leap of faith? Why? Why not?

Yes. Should we be willing to take a daily leap? Is life about comfort? If we will see beyond ourselves and seek to use what we have been given for benefit beyond ourselves we are making an investment in life itself. Life is too precious to be spent, it should be invested.

Q For what are you waiting? Why are you waiting?

I may have been waiting for things to be almost perfect, just right. Moving to Portland, Oregon, has helped indirectly as it often rains. Since I love to be outdoors, I bought rain gear and go out whenever time permits. Weather has no permit!

I am waiting to be sure the move is what God would have.

Q Are you ambitious for something? Do you have ambition to something? What is the difference in life between being ambitious for something and having ambition to something? What value do you place on ambition?

I have ambition to learn, grow and be who I'm given to be, to live the dreams and the vision that the purpose is fulfilled. An ambition for something will bind you to the something. Ambition to something will move you in life, will be a motive force to learn. The value of ambition is proportionately related to the degree to which one connects it to growing with life, being productive in one's purpose all life long.

Q Do you compete? Do you compete against others? With yourself? Why? What is the difference in terms of direction in life?

If I compete it is with myself, not with others. Competing with others means you are applying yourself only to what already exists. Where is the exploration and where are the possibilities?

You will never know wholly who you are if you use someone else as a measuring stick. Why set a course measured against others, a course already run? In fact, why run? Is it a race? And, from another perspective, why not choose flying, soaring? If you focus on competing against another, how will you uncover who you are and what you have been given to give, your lightest self? If you don't set out to uncover your instrument how will your music ever be played? How can it sound the heights? Would you arrive at the end not knowing who you really are and then remain buried in earth?

Q What is the difference in terms of direction in life between a focus on competing and a focus beyond what currently exists?

A focus on competing is a focus on what currently exists. Competing is an unseen contract to merely maintain or improve within existing frameworks. A focus beyond what exists is an offer to soar with our dreams. We give too much weight to external references when we look to compete and we set ourselves up to miss the far more important reference, the source, oneself as created for a specific purpose. The difference is the right direction, pursuing your true purpose, or the wrong direction. The wrong direction means never uncovering purpose, never really knowing who you are and therefore not realizing the gift given because you were looking the wrong way. That is, you were looking at someone else, a mechanical, manmade notion, a measuring stick, instead of looking inwards and beyond. It's a choice. Would you rather look only within the realm of what already exists or to what can be—who you can be and the whole realm of Possibilities, to what life is meant to be?

A story . . .
This makes me think of Pete Sampras. I love tennis, playing and watching tennis. One year I decided to take my vacation and watch a week's worth of the ATP tour in Cincinnati.

Early each morning I would go to the smaller courts where the players all practice before their games and where the games leading up to the final at week's end take place. Almost everyday I got to see Pete, along with Rafter, Agassi, Kafelnikov and others play. For years I had been enjoying seeing these players on television, and particularly Pete. It was very interesting to be able to see a player's game one day and how it changed on another day. Even more interesting was seeing a player in his stride play a great game and then get on the court with Pete. What was it about playing Pete that threw everybody off? Even when Pete was not in his stride, Agassi and Rafter for example, who might be having a really good day, were thrown. Were they intimidated? It was something about Pete, not even his game, just walking on the court with him that got to them. It wasn't something you could "see." It was much deeper than that. Pete didn't compete. He was so very competitive but he didn't compete. He had decided years before that he was going down in the history books of tennis. When he stepped on the court he was playing his game, moving his game with the long view in sight. The fellow across the net had nothing to do with it. Every time Pete stepped on the big court in the Slams he wasn't just playing to win the game, he was playing for history.

When the vision is beyond what exists in the moment there is a momentum in our action that has the advantage, having been built far beyond the moment, of power from a foundation un-rocked by current goings on, and therefore is not of this time or for someone in the moment to stop.

Q Have you uncovered your purpose?

Yes, it is very clear that my purpose is under God and therefore I look to him for my vision.

Q Are you uncovering your visions?

The visions for life have been and are being uncovered. On the surface; starting a business, helping create something new, a publication in an area that didn't formerly exist, moving to the United States, living in California and in New York, acting in film and theatre, reeducating in the dramatic arts. More substantially the visions led to working with different groups of people, people who approached life linearly and those who approached life creatively. This has meant being able to learn about people and what our approach means for the way life may be lived. This experience led to creating dialogue and real learning.

Q What is the difference between a vision and a goal?

A goal we make up. It is in the realm of the short term. A vision is already ours, created beyond ourselves, and to be uncovered. As we uncover our purpose, our visions come into focus.

Q What is the difference between vision and purpose?

We have one purpose in life and it is our responsibility to uncover it. Our purpose is for the long term and is eternal. While in one sense our purpose is given us, we must also choose it. Then our visions for life begin to unfold and come into focus. Purpose is the deep underlying current in our lives and it is our responsibility to fathom the depths. As we move in life and our visions are realized, our underlying purpose moves us forward to the next vision. Purpose is as the current in the stream. As we board our boat our vision may be our friend's landing. We moor and visit our friend and our vision is realized. We board our boat again and it is our purpose that carries us forward to the next vision. Visions are the concrete manifestations arising out of purpose.

Q What was the difference between Churchill and Hitler?

Have you considered their names? One was for the reality of life and freedom. One was for himself and his power without respect for his maker. One understood that life is created as a gift to us, that it is our responsibility to care for it as given. One saw life to be used to his own ends and, therefore, left destruction in his wake. One's motives were good, the others evil. Hitler saw as J. K. Rowling has the character of Voldomort see, "There is no good and evil, only power and those too weak to use it."

Q What differentiates lives?

Our deepest held beliefs. From a belief in God comes the knowledge that love is eternal. From this we can know that the love we give here and are given will not die when we die to this life. From this comes knowing that you, and by extrapolation others, have a purpose. This leads to the provision for uncovering that purpose for life, of uncovering who we are given to be. This leads to true and lasting relationships and a productive life. Belief in God has us look long term, leads us to the eternal. All else is but the shallows.

Q Is there good and evil?

Yes, most evidently by looking for example to the motives of Churchill and Hitler. It is our responsibility to see the lie, that there is no good and evil. If we will not take responsibility to see clearly, we obscure the truth and weaken our ability to act upon it. If we will not face reality we threaten our freedom to make this very choice and freedom now and for posterity.

Q Is life worth moving from a short-term to a long-term perspective?

This question has full impact on all of life. It helps determine whether we spend or invest our time. It impacts the decision about with whom we spend or invest our time, what we stop doing, start and focus upon, on who we aspire to be. If we don't take the time, to do the thinking now, neither do we taste the sweetness of the ripe fruit. Then at the end, who will we be when there is no more time? Will you accept the end you find, and as final? Or are you meant for much more?

Q What questions would you ask?

Index

Karen Proctor is the founder of NewThink, where she works in dialogue and real learning with her clients. She is also founder of *Energizer Magazine* and a co-founder of The Mint Theatre in New York City. Karen lives in Portland, Oregon and Calgary, Alberta. She may be reached at karenproctor@newthinkfyb.com.